CONTENTS

PRINTED IN   GREAT BRITAIN
DEAN & SON Ltd.
52/54 Southwark St.   LONDON SE1 1UA
TRADE MARK

Day by Day

Stories about David

Stories retold by Virginia Williams-Ellis
Illustrated by Harry Bishop

© Dean & Son Ltd., 1981
ISBN 0-603-00273-0

David the Shepherd Boy

David was a shepherd boy in the days of King Saul. He lived in Bethlehem with his father, Jesse, and his seven brothers.

Each day he went out to the fields beyond the town and stayed there until evening, looking after his father's sheep. Often this was dangerous work. Fierce wild animals lived in the hills. Sometimes a bear or lion would come down into the fields to kill one of the sheep. David had to be very brave. He had learnt how to kill a wild animal with a stone. He would choose a large round stone, place it in his leather sling and whirl it above his head. The stone would fly out and hit the animal on the head. David always looked after his flock of sheep well and kept them safe.

In the evenings, when he had finished his work, David loved to play his harp. He could play happily for hours and the music he made was so beautiful that many people had heard about him. He was a kind and handsome boy, and loved by all who knew him.

God had chosen David determined that one day he should become King over the whole land of Israel. So God sent His servant, the priest Samuel, to Jesse's house. David was brought before Samuel, and Samuel poured oil on David's head as a sign that he was specially chosen by God.

One day, when David was working in the fields, a messenger from his father's house came running out to find him.

'You are to leave the sheep,' he told David, 'and come home quickly. King Saul has sent for you!'

'What can the King want me for?' David exclaimed.

He hurried back into Bethlehem. One of the King's servants was waiting for him.

'King Saul has heard how beautifully you play the harp. He is unwell and he has ordered you to come and play for him.'

So David packed his harp and set out for Jerusalem.

When David arrived at the palace he was taken immediately to King Saul. The King was lying on a couch, scowling. He did not look up.

'Play to me!' he ordered.

David could see that the King was not ill, but very unhappy. He took up his harp and, choosing a quiet, soothing tune, he played to the King for a long time.

After a while Saul looked up and began to watch David. He watched his quiet, happy face and his fingers moving across the strings. The music relaxed him and he began to feel much better.

'You play very well,' the King said when David had finished. 'I shall ask your father to let you become my armour-bearer. Then you will be able to play for me whenever I need you.'

After this David often left his home to stay at the palace and he became the King's favourite servant.

1 SAMUEL, chapter 16

David and Goliath

David's three oldest brothers were all soldiers in King Saul's army. Saul was fighting a war against the Philistines.

One day Jesse said to David:

'Go to the camp and find out how your brothers are. Take them these ten loaves and some cheese for their captain and bring me back a token that all is going well.'

Early next day David set out with the parcels of food. When he arrived at the camp he found everybody very excited. The army was already moving out towards the battlefield. David left his parcels in the camp and ran into the midst of the soldiers. At last he found his brothers. He talked with them excitedly about the coming battle.

Suddenly a cry went up from the Philistines. David looked across the battlefield and saw a huge man step out from the Philistine army. He was ten feet tall and wore an enormous brass helmet and a heavy suit of armour.

'Who is that?' David asked his brothers.

'That is Goliath of Gath!' his brothers told him. 'He has challenged anyone from our army to fight him in single combat. If he is killed the Philistines will be our slaves. Otherwise we must become their slaves. Of course nobody dares take up the challenge!'

'Nobody dares!' cried David. 'How dare Goliath treat the people of God like this. I will fight him!'

David went to see King Saul.

'You couldn't kill Goliath,' said Saul. 'You're only a boy!'

'God has helped me to kill bears and lions,' David told him. 'He will help me kill Goliath too.'

In the end Saul agreed to let David go. He gave him a suit of armour. David put it on, but he could hardly move in it.

'This is much too heavy for me,' he said. 'I will wear just my shepherd's clothes and take my sling and some stones.'

David found five smooth stones and put them in his bag. Then he walked confidently out onto the battlefield. Both the armies watched, amazed. Goliath strode across the field in all his armour and with his shield-bearer ahead of him.

'Who do you think I am?' Goliath roared mockingly, when he saw that David had no weapons. 'Do you think you can beat me with a stick?'

'You come to me with a sword,' said David calmly, 'but I come to you in the name of the living God!'

Then David took a stone, placed it in his sling, and whirled the sling above his head. The stone flew through the air and hit Goliath on his forehead. He fell to the ground.

King Saul's army cheered. David ran to where Goliath lay and cut off his head. When the Philistines saw that their great champion was dead, they turned and fled.

David was taken to King Saul.

'You have saved Israel!' said Saul. 'You must stay at the court as a captain in my army.'

1 SAMUEL, chapter 17

David and Jonathan

King Saul had a son called Jonathan. He was a handsome boy. Jonathan liked David very much. He was overjoyed when he heard that David was going to live at the palace.

'My father, the King, says he will treat you like his own son,' Jonathan said to David, 'so we will be like brothers to each other.'

The boys clasped hands as a sign of their friendship.

'And we will always stand by one another,' said David, 'whatever happens to us.'

Jonathan then gave David one of his own robes to wear, his belt and sword, and his bow and arrows.

'I am giving you these,' Jonathan told David solemnly, 'to show you that I will always be your friend.'

After David had killed Goliath there was great rejoicing in Israel. The streets were full of people dancing and singing and playing musical instruments. All the people cried:

'King Saul has killed thousands, but David has killed tens of thousands of the enemy!'

Everybody wanted to see David, the brave shepherd boy. When King Saul heard the people shouting for David he suddenly became very jealous.

'Soon my people will be wanting David as their King instead of me,' he thought. 'I must find a way to kill him.'

At first Saul hoped that David would be killed in battle.

The Israelites were still at war with the Philistines and David often had to lead his men to fight. But David was a good leader and always won the battles that he fought.

So Saul called his counsellors and his son Jonathan.

'This young man, David, is turning my people against me,' he told them. 'I order you to have him murdered at once!'

Jonathan was very worried when he heard this. He warned David. Then as soon as he could he spoke to his father alone.

'Father,' he pleaded, 'David is a good person. He has never done you any wrong. If you kill him you will always be sorry.'

Saul listened as his son reasoned with him.

'You are right,' he said at last. 'I was wrong to be jealous. I will not do your friend any harm.'

Jonathan told David that King Saul was no longer angry, and David returned to the court.

One day, when King Saul was in one of his blackest moods, he called David to play the harp to him. As usual David sat at Saul's feet. But this time the music did not soothe the King. As Saul watched the handsome boy, he was overcome again with jealousy. Suddenly, leaping to his feet, the King seized a spear and hurled it at David.

David saw the spear flying towards him and dodged out of its way. It struck the wall just beside him. David ran from the room. He knew now that Saul was still very angry with him. The King would never be satisfied until David was dead.

1 SAMUEL, chapters 18, 19

David Flees from Saul

David found Jonathan and told him what had happened.

'What have I done to anger your father?' he asked.

Jonathan was very sad that his father hated David so much.
'I will find out if the King is sorry for what he did,' he
promised. 'Go out and hide in the fields. In three days I will
come to tell you if it is safe to return to the court.'

Three days later David went to the place where he had
promised to meet Jonathan. Soon he saw his friend coming
towards him across the fields.

'My father is still angry,' said Jonathan. 'It is not safe for
you to go back to the palace.'

'Goodbye, then,' said David sadly. 'I must leave you.'

'You have been my best friend,' Jonathan said. 'I will try to
prevent my father from doing you any harm.'

The boys shook hands. Then Jonathan returned to the city
and David set off into the wilderness.

David's friends heard that he was hiding from Saul and
they went to find him. Soon more than four hundred men
had gathered to protect him. They set up a camp in the
woods.

One day David's men came to him with some news:

'King Saul has come to look for you! He has brought an
army of three thousand men, and they are camped nearby!'

'You must not worry,' David said. 'God will protect us.'

Nabal and Abigail

Not far from David's camp there was a sheep farm owned by a very rich man called Nabal. Nabal was mean and bad-tempered, but he had a wife, Abigail, who was an understanding woman and very beautiful.

One day David heard that Nabal was shearing his sheep. This was a very festive time of year for the farmers. David sent ten of his young men to Nabal with a special message.

'We bring good wishes to you, from David, our leader,' they said. 'We have been living with your shepherds out in the fields and have helped them protect the flock. And though we were sometimes hungry we have never taken any of your sheep. Now that it is shearing time we hoped you might share with us a little of the feast you are preparing.'

'Who is this man David,' Nabal asked angrily, 'to come asking for gifts? If I give you some of the food from the feast there won't be enough for us! Be off with you!'

When David heard what Nabal had said he was very angry.

'Put on your swords,' he ordered his men, 'and come with me! We shall kill Nabal and every one of his men!'

Now one of Nabal's shepherds had heard David's message and he told Nabal's wife, Abigail, about their request, and Nabal's angry response.

'These men have always been good to us when we were out with them in the fields. They should be thanked for what

they have done. There may be trouble otherwise.'

Abigail was very sorry that her husband had treated David so unkindly. Quickly she prepared a feast for his men. She strapped the parcels of food onto the backs of her donkeys. Then, without telling her husband, she set off on one of the donkeys, while her servant led the others on ahead of her.

As they travelled down the hill they saw David and his men coming towards them. Abigail dismounted quickly.

'My lord,' she said, bowing to David. 'I have come to say sorry for the way my husband treated you. If I had seen your messengers I would have gladly given you all you asked. But God is with you, and has kept you from harming anyone. You would have been sorry later had you killed anybody. Please accept these gifts which I have brought you.'

'Bless the Lord God of Israel for sending you to meet me,' David replied, 'and may He bless you for stopping me from harming anyone. Thank you for your generous gifts. Return home to your husband now. You need not fear us.'

When Nabal heard how Abigail had taken the food to David, and what David had been about to do, he was so shocked he became like a stone, was very ill, and never recovered. Ten days later he died.

David heard of Nabal's death and later he sent messengers to ask Abigail to marry him. Abigail agreed. Taking five of her serving girls with her she left her home and returned with the messengers to become David's wife.

1 SAMUEL, chapter 25

David, King of Israel

King Saul was still at war with the Philistines, but his armies were now very weak. During one battle the Philistines killed almost all the Israelites. Then they found and killed three of Saul's sons. One of these was Jonathan, David's friend. Last of all they overtook King Saul on the battlefield. One of the Philistine archers shot him with an arrow. Saul fell to the ground, groaning. He was very badly wounded.

'Kill me with your sword,' the King ordered his armour-bearer, 'before I am captured by the enemy.'

But the armour-bearer was too frightened to kill the King. So Saul put the point of his own sword against his heart and fell upon it. Saul, King of Israel, was dead.

It was three days before David heard about the battle. A soldier, tired, dirty and with his clothes torn, arrived at the place where David was living.

'Tell me everything that happened in the battle,' David urged the man.

'The Israelite army has been defeated,' the soldier told him. 'Thousands of our men are dead and wounded. And both Saul and Jonathan were killed.'

David was overcome with grief. He had lost Jonathan, his greatest friend. And though Saul had treated him so badly, David had always loved him too. David wrote a song in honour of his friends:

'How are the mighty fallen,' he sang,
'Saul and Jonathan were lovely and pleasant in their lives,
And in their death they were not divided.
They were swifter than eagles,
They were stronger than lions. . .
How are the mighty fallen in the midst of the battle.'

After Saul's death David was crowned as the new King, just as God had ordained so many years before. God was with him in all he did and he tried to rule his country by God's laws.

David ruled Israel for forty years. When he was a very old man God chose David's son, Solomon, to become King after his death. The name Solomon means 'peaceful'. During David's reign there had been many wars, but God promised that when Solomon ruled there would be peace in Israel.

'God has chosen you, during your reign of peace, to build a great Temple for Him which will be famous throughout the world,' David told Solomon, 'but I will help you plan it.'

King David had collected all the materials to build the Temple, and great treasures to decorate it.

'Remember,' David said, 'all these things are given us by God. We are only giving back to Him what is His already.'

After David's death King Solomon hired the most skilful craftsmen in the country. Together they built the largest and most beautiful Temple ever seen.

1 SAMUEL, chapter 31, 2 SAMUEL, chapter 1, 1 CHRONICLES, chapters 22, 28, 29, 2 CHRONICLES, chapters 1, 2